Discovering The World Around Us

Extra-Ordinary ELEPHANTS
Cool and Interesting Facts

TJ Rob

Extra-Ordinary Elephants
Cool and Interesting Facts
By TJ Rob

From the Discovering The World Around Us Series, Volume 1

© Copyright Text TJ Rob, 2015

All rights reserved. No part of the book may be reproduced in any form without permission in writing from the author. Reviewers may quote brief passages in review.

ISBN 978-1-988695-03-7

Disclaimer

No part of this book may be reproduced in any form or by any means, mechanical or electronic, including photocopying or recording, or by an information storage and retrieval system, or transmitted by email without permission in writing from the publisher. This book is for entertainment purposes only. The views expressed are those of author alone.

Published by
TJ Rob
Suite 609
440-10816 Macleod Trail SE
Calgary, AB T2J 5N8 www.TJRob.com

Photo Credits: All images used under license from Fotolia.com

back cover, Dmitry Pichugin; front cover, KYSLYNSKYY EDUARD; pg 1, Dmitry Pichugin; pg 2, Dmitry Pichugin; pg 3, Dmitry Pichugin; pg 4, Steve Allen; pg 5, Steve Allen; pg 6, Gualtiero Boffi; pg 6, eyetronic; pg 6, photosvac; pg 7, eyetronic; pg 7, kdreams02; pg 8, lantapix; pg 9, zanarinilara ; pg 10, David STeele; pg 11, David STeele; pg 12, gallas; pg 13, Nico Smit; pg 13, Alta Oosthuizen; pg 14, obiahman; pg 15, obiahman; pg 17, topten22photo; pg 18, miroslav_1 ; pg 19, miroslav_1 ; pg 20, Alta Oosthuizen; pg 22, Steve Allen; pg 23, Nico Smit; pg 24, Worakit Sirijinda; pg 25, sidliks; pg 26, SunnyS; pg 27, G du Prez; pg 28, pict rider; pg 29, Nico Smit; pg 29, onot; pg 29, lucaar; pg 30, Marie-Anne Aberson Meijers; pg 31, Marie-Anne Aberson Meijers; pg 32, jodie777; pg 33, Dominique LUZY; pg 34, Martina Berg; pg 35, Martina Berg; pg 37, metalaxiz ; pg 39, Artush

Table of Contents	Page
How much does an Elephant weigh?	6
What are the different types of Elephant?	7
Where do you find Elephants?	8
How long do Elephants live?	9
How do wild Elephants live together?	10
Do Elephants have feelings?	14
What about Elephant babies?	16
What do Elephants eat?	20
What do Elephants use their trunks for?	22
Do Elephants have a good sense of smell?	24
How well do Elephants sleep?	25
What about Tusks?	26
Are Elephants scared of Mice	28
Thick Wrinkly Skin	29
How fast can Elephants move?	30
Big Soft Feet	32
Big Ears	33
Do Elephants love water?	34
How do Elephants communicate with each other?	36
Are Elephants smart?	38

Elephants are the world's biggest land animals.

They have been on Earth for the last 5 to 6 million years. Longer than us humans.

Keep reading and you will learn what amazing creatures they are!

How much does 1 adult Elephant weigh?

The same weight as 2 Rhinos OR 20 Lions.

  2 Rhinos

20 Lions (Only 5 are shown here)

What are the different types of Elephant?

African Elephants

Asian Elephants

African Elephants are bigger and heavier than Asian Elephants.

The African Elephant has bigger ears too.

Both male and female African Elephants have tusks.

Only some Asian males have tusks.

Where do Wild Elephants Live?

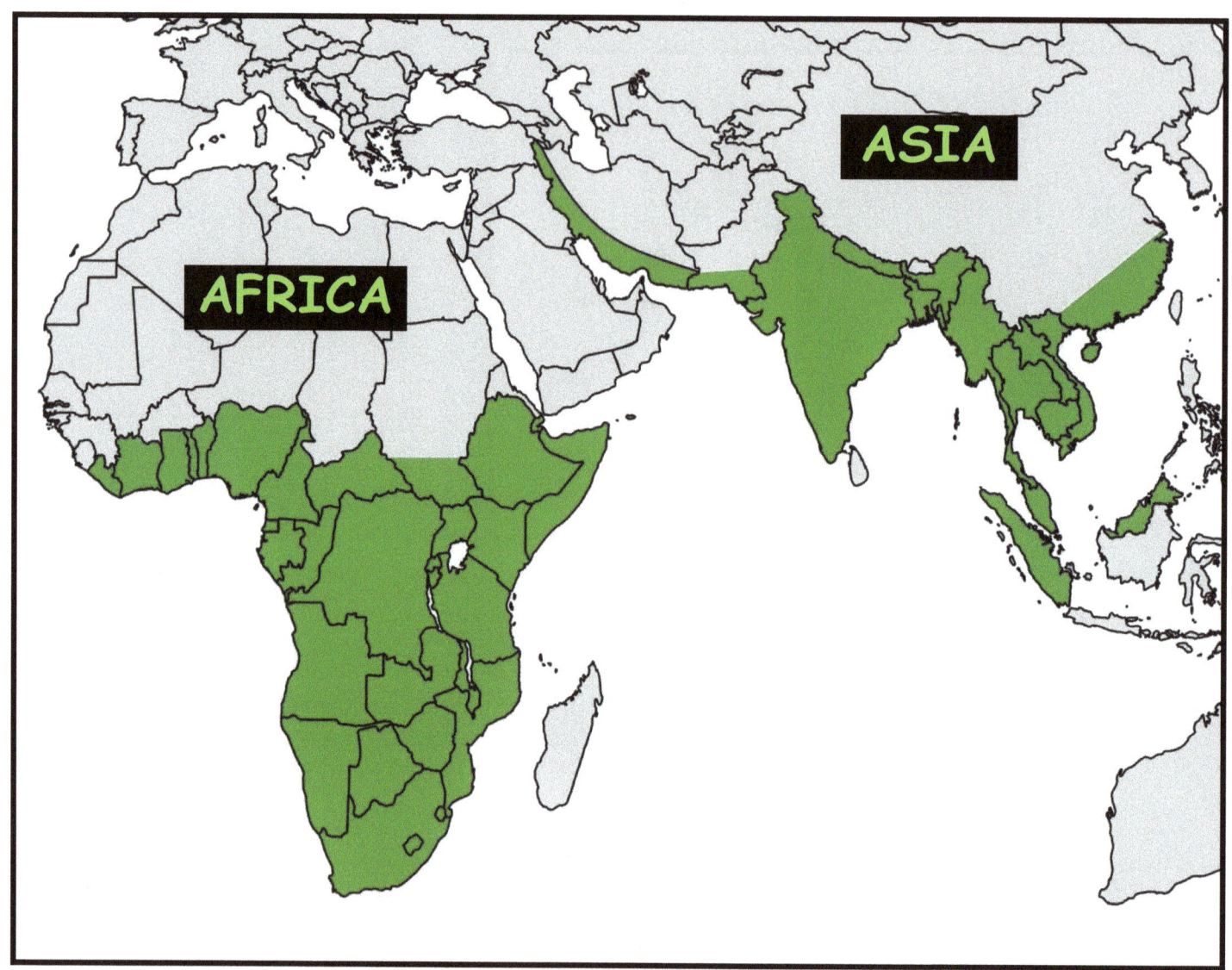

Africa — between 450,000 to 700,000 Wild Elephants

Asia — between 35,000 to 45,000 Wild Elephants

How long do Elephants Live?

Elephants can live a long time.

Many live until they are 70 years old.

The oldest known Elephant was 86 years old!

How do Wild Elephants live together?

Elephants of all ages live in herds of up to 25 Elephants.

The leader of the herd is normally an older female Elephant called the matriarch.

She decides when it's time for the herd to move, where they will go to next and when they should rest.

The males leave the herd when they reach about 12 years old and join other young males in a male herd of their own.

Adult male Elephants are called bulls or bull Elephants. Bulls are the largest of all Elephants.

When they grow older the males split away from the male herd and live alone.

Elephants are very social animals

They greet each other to say "hello".

They love to play.

Do Elephants have feelings?

Elephants are highly sensitive creatures.
When a baby Elephant is upset or complains the whole herd comes over to help it.

They will help and feed a hurt or fallen Elephant. Just like humans, Elephants get sad when a loved one dies, or when someone that they were close to, dies.

What about Elephant babies?

A baby Elephant is called a calf.

A calf can stand on its feet shortly after being born.

A calf can weigh 250 pounds (113 kg) at birth — more than some of the biggest football players.

30 human babies would be the same weight as 1 baby Elephant.

A Female Elephant is called a Cow.

Cows can have calves every 4 to 5 years.

Over their lifetime, a Cow normally will have 4 to 5 calves, but up to 12 has been recorded.

Cows have a 22 month long pregnancy. The longest pregnancy of all animals.

A Human pregnancy is much shorter at 9 months.

What do Elephants eat?

They love to eat grasses, small bushes and plants, green leaves, fruit, roots, bark and twigs.

Elephants eat for up to 16 hours a day.

They eat over 300 pounds (340 kg) of food a day.

That's like us eating over 150 plates of food in a single day!

Elephants also drink about 50 gallons (190 liters) of water every day – about the same amount as filling your bathtub to the very top!

What do Elephants use their trunks for?

Elephants use their trunks to breathe and make noises like trumpeting.

They also use their trunks to feel and understand the size and shape of things.

Most importantly, they use their trunks to suck up water to put in their mouths to drink.

Their trunks are so sensitive they can pick up a single blade of grass.

The trunk is filled with thousands of tiny muscles.

This allows the trunk to move in all directions and also makes it very strong.

They are also so strong they can lift up huge logs and trees that weigh up to 750 pounds (340 kg).

Do Elephants have a good sense of smell?

With such a long trunk, Elephants have one of the best sense of smell of all animals.

They can smell water more than 10 miles (16 km) away.

They lift their trunks and swing them from side to side to smell better.

How well do Elephants sleep?

Compared to dogs, Elephants hardly sleep at all.

Every day dogs sleep from 12 to 14 hours.

Elephants get only 4 hours of sleep a night.

What about Tusks?

Elephants start to grow their tusks from the age of between 2 to 3 years old.

Tusks are not made of bone but of ivory.

Tusks never stop growing throughout the entire life of the Elephant, just like your finger nails.

If a tusk is broken off at the root it cannot grow back.

Elephants use their tusks to defend themselves.

They also use them for digging and lifting and moving objects.

Just like humans are right or left handed, Elephants also prefer one tusk over another.

Are Elephants scared of Mice?

Elephants are not scared of mice.

Elephants are scared of bees.

They know a swarm of bees can get up their super sensitive trunks and sting them.

Thick Wrinkly Skin

Even though an Elephant has a thick skin it still can get sunburnt.

So they use sand and mud like sunscreen to protect their skins.

Their skin is so sensitive Elephants can feel a fly landing on them!

This Page looks just like Elephant skin

How fast can Elephants move?

Elephants can't run like we do. They are too heavy.

They can walk fast and cover long distances.

Some have been known to move at 25 miles per hour (40 km per hour) for short distances.

They are great walkers and can easily cover 50 miles (80 km) in a single day.

Big Soft Feet

Elephants have soft padding under the soles of their feet.

This helps to cushion their huge weight every time they take a step.

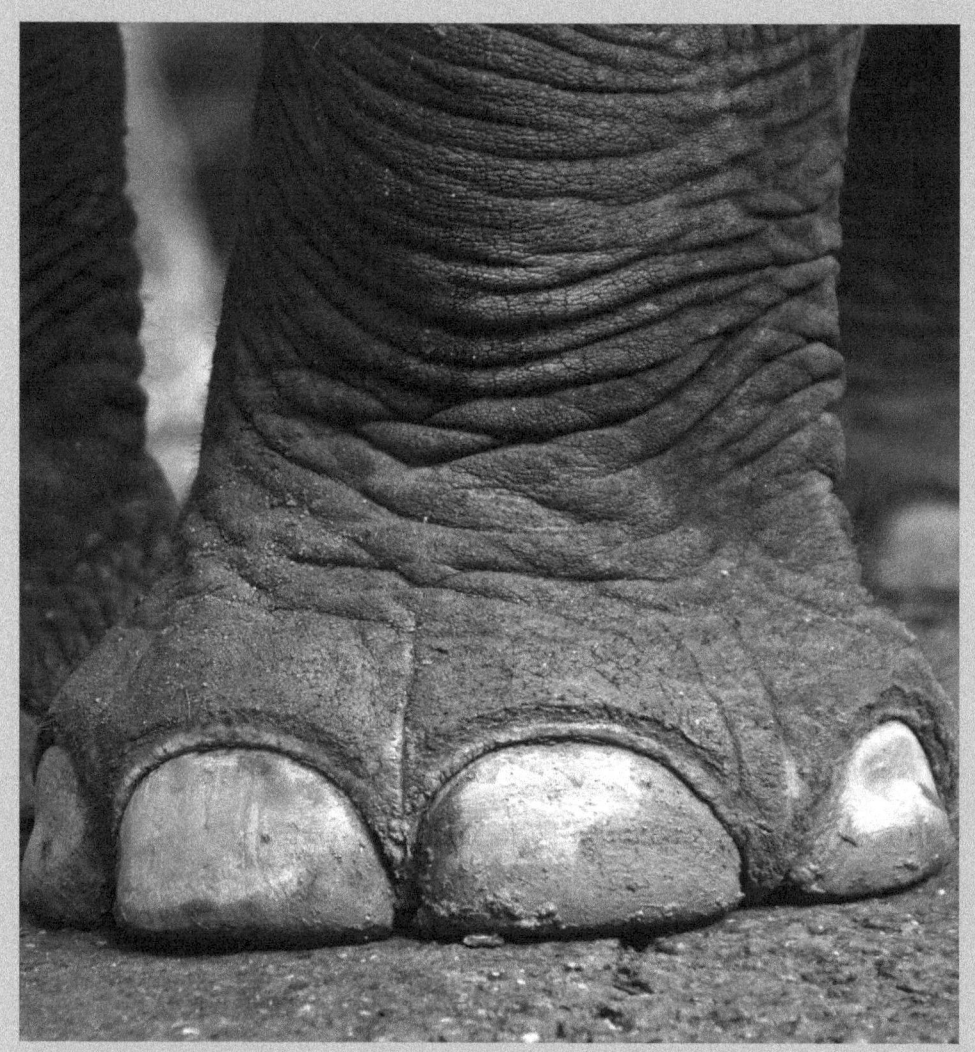

The soft padding also helps them feel where they are going.

It also quietens any sound. Elephants can walk so silently that you can barely hear them.

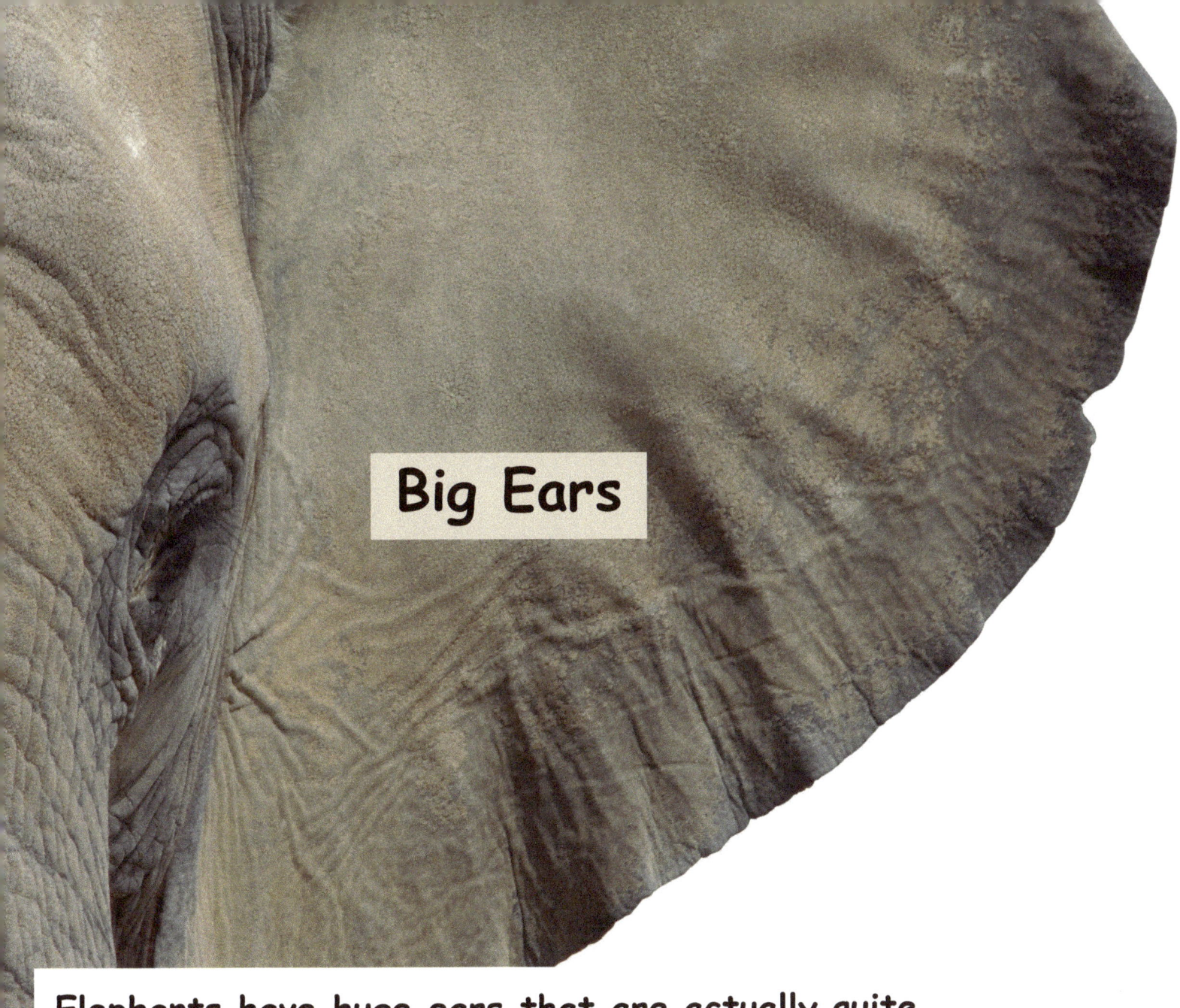

Big Ears

Elephants have huge ears that are actually quite thin.

They are filled with blood vessels that help them cool off.

Elephants have really good hearing.

They can hear sounds from miles away.

They also flap their ears to scare off other animals and people.

Elephants love water.

They love to play in water and it helps keep them cool.

Do Elephants love water?

Elephants can swim. They lift their trunks out of the water and use them like snorkels so they can breathe.

How do Elephants communicate with each other?

Elephants make a low rumbling sound that vibrates in the ground to communicate with each other.

Many of these sounds are beyond the range of hearing of humans.

Elephants often listen for this rumbling sound by putting their trunks on the ground to feel the vibrations of the sound with their trunks.

They also can feel this rumbling sound with their sensitive feet.

Other Elephants can hear these rumbling sounds from miles away.

Are Elephants smart?

"An Elephant never forgets" - smart with an amazing memory.

Elephants can remember other animals, people, and events from years before.

They remember places like water holes and routes to food even when they don't go to them for long periods of time.

Elephants are able to understand and remember more than 60 commands.

Like humans, Elephants can recognize themselves in a mirror.

THANKS FOR READING!

Please leave a review at the website where you bought this book and tell others what you liked about it.

Visit www.TJRob.com for a FREE eBook and to see TJ Rob's other exciting books

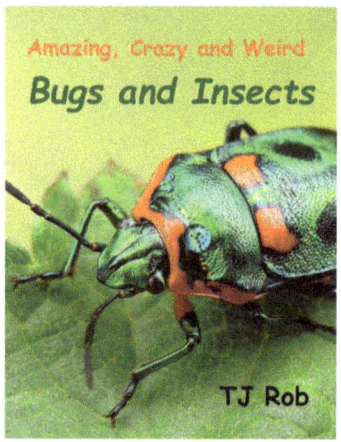

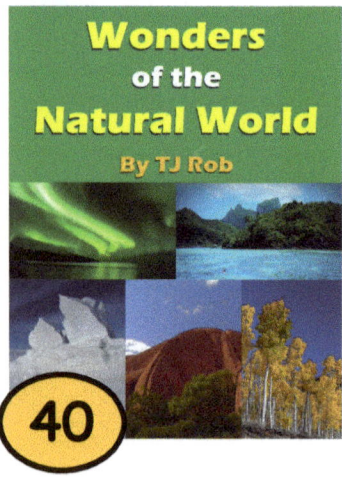
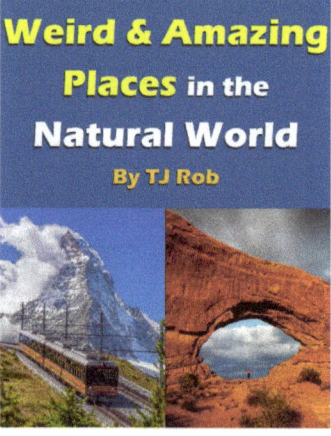

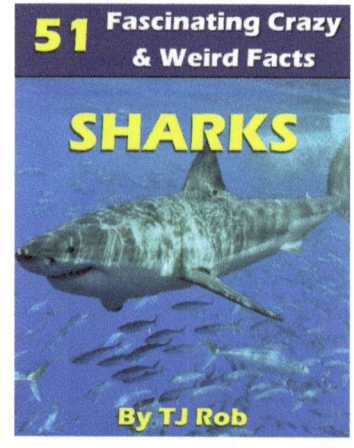